UNLESS ACTED UPON

UNLESS ACTED UPON

Tim Conley

Mansfield Press

Library and Archives Canada Cataloguing in Publication

Title: Unless acted upon / Tim Conley.
Names: Conley, Tim, 1972- author.
Description: Poems.
Identifiers: Canadiana 20190102608 | ISBN 9781771262125 (softcover)
Classification: LCC PS8605.O56 U55 2019 | DDC C811/.54—dc23

Cover Image: Tim Conley
Author Photo: Alice Callas
Design: Denis De Klerck

The publication of *Unless Acted Upon* has been generously supported by
the Canada Council for the Arts and the Ontario Arts Council.

Mansfield Press Inc.
25 Mansfield Avenue, Toronto, Ontario, Canada M6J 2A9
Publisher: Denis De Klerck
www.mansfieldpress.net

First as trickery, then as force

CONTENTS

These contigencies are all around
us: under our hats, affixing them to
our troubled heads; across the skies,

playing nice with strato-nimbus and
company; carrying fragile betrayals
to their destinations, let these sound

waves unobstructed go; mixing soup
with nuts, triggering the allergy or
something quite like it; pushing and

pulling us to better, you had better,
is that better, what on earth is better.
Let's say there might be laws of

emotion, because isn't emotion a
combo of magnitude and direction?
The torque and tension of our talks

late into the repeated nights, weight
and friction, push and pull, beloved
acrobat, the feelings felt defining ours.

SLAPSTICK I

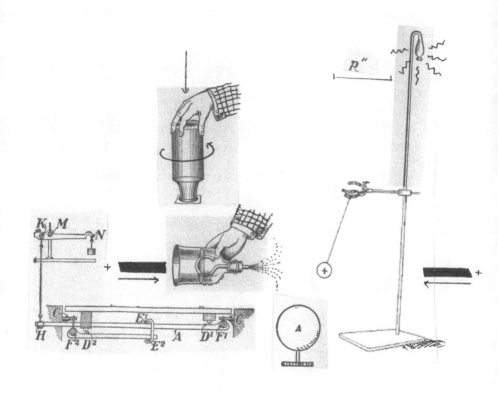

Fig. 26. Confounding the divine afflatus.

NOT EXACTLY RUNNING AWAY FROM HOME

Happiness is not a scalar and you will get nowhere pretending that it is. Gestures can be both spectacular and piacular, given the wrong moment. I wonder what I did with your number.

Reciprocity would make an excellent name for a roller coaster. There is up, there is way up, and there is way up high. Do you suppose that there might be energies that cannot be measured?

Stasis is an affair of doilies and placemats. No coincidence that the most prominent feature on that urban nomad's bicycle is the rear-view mirror. It can be hard to tell when you're joking.

The trouble starts when basic principles take a leave of absence. Certain doors nearly require slamming to close and send unintentional messages. It's not that I don't get lost in thought.

What zones want is everybody on the same page. So long as there is a solid connection, none of the other team is going to break through. You don't have to answer if you're preoccupied.

GWELI

They have found the gene
that compels you to read
this poem. In it dwell an
untroubled couple who
sleep separately. Though they
have not discussed it, both
of them are much taken
with a song heard on the
radio, a song that includes
some memorable phrase
or other, people used to be
heard humming it while they
waited for the bus or set
to adjusting stubborn shower
nozzles. It's not abulia, by
the way: file that search
engine result away with all
of the bad guesses that stand
in for happiness. Cain,
don't rise up, don't float
away, don't give up on
the light of the dying rage,
but think of the opposite
of bus schedules. None of
this makes anyone any more
or less vulnerable (the Welsh
word for wound is *gweli*, you
cannot pretend that you don't
enjoy it, *gweli*). People are
talking about other people,
but these words are yours, they
are talking to you, and it
doesn't matter, in fact it
never mattered who else was

in the room. Genetic data
are not only reliable but hey,
the only game in town, dig?
Poke fun, fun has been well
and truly poked. Is it a far,
far better thing we do now?
No need to give the nod, it's
given. Disagree somewhat,
disagree, strongly disagree.

SNAGGED

Not our time, you said, and it wasn't,
it was hardly the time, it was just barely,
that one time. Unziploc'd, arced over,
then a bus to catch, a bus to be caught.

Hands scented with antiquarian pages
and youth, I am someone's trophy trout
still twisting on the line. Why not do
both, you said, and I could not see

why not. Nothing easier. Optometrist
father must have given you those eyes,
I must never have said, done but not
doing. It is not our time. And I ashore
once more.

GLANCING BLOWS

Didn't you have kind of a thing for Ming
the Merciless' daughter? And if you didn't,
why didn't you? We're talking about a
different colour of blood here. Don't say

you're not interested. Hang on, you can't
park here: can't you see it's reserved? Why
do you play just that one string on the, on
the banjo, is it? You can see what humidity

does, eternal gratitude notwithstanding, to
one's memory, make a note of that. Weren't
you holding my hand? And if you weren't,
why weren't you? Anything can be forgiven

if the radio works. No harm leaving the back
door open when there are no burglars. What
did you expect? That everyone would drop
everything and sing along? Try convincing

the attendant. Your disk cleanup will surely
be your undoing. Didn't we already talk about
all of this? Please don't slip your head into
that fake noose. Didn't you, didn't I do that?

DECLENSIONS

I

What she does with her knuckles, what the differences in height give my neck, what sounds stream from the spawning bed, what amphibious releases, what thieves of uncounted sheep, what everything depends upon.

What undoes the smile, what we pray don't rise, what gives away the intruder, what eventual passing does not sound like, what are held by shepherds, what needs resolution.

II

When it is given and seen to be given, when it reminds one of another, when it is bountiful, when it tastes of defeat, when it is covertly revealed, when it is just a matter of that.

When the light falls where necessary, when it is not the contrary, when it is great but still, when it's sprung and does its thing, when it turns.

COBWEB

...language attaches to envelops its referent without destroying
or changing it—the way a cobweb catches a fly.
Susan Howe, *The Quarry*

Not much of sticky point, the possible
lingering distinction between what the
artful spider makes and the tendrils
of dust that seem without a maker, self-
accreting, pointless, harmless even to
a fly. Not much, but in as much as
undone housework amounts to a real
archive, there's reason to wonder what
level of *musca domestica* subintelligence
is needed to fall for these things, or,
in other words, what on earth are we
thinking when we allow ourselves to
mean exactly what's being said? Not
mouche, judges the wordless spider,
for whom none of this is a problem.

HOLDING PATTERN

my tongue
if the wisdom is plain enough;

your fire
if you will trust me to do so;

if you have to be somewhere don't let me

FORCE, ARBITRARY USE OF

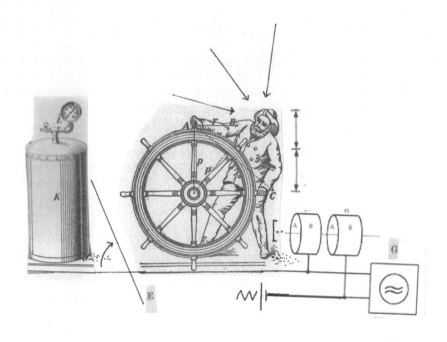

Fig. 58. Resistance to PR pressure.

AUTHORITIES ASK TO HEAR FROM

anyone who may have seen anything
anyone who has further information
anyone who has any information

anyone with any special insights
anyone with a definite plan of action
anyone for whom inaction can sometimes be the rightest action

anyone whose sense of justice includes mercy and humour
anyone who knows that help is both a verb and a noun but also a way of living
anyone who understands the nature and value of dialogue

anyone who is honest and unafraid of tenderness
anyone who brings stability and security to a relationship
anyone hurt but willing to go on, knowing that to go on is to be hurt again

anyone who prefers to remember things as faulty human memory preserves them
anyone who begs leave to doubt Carly Simon's exegesis of her own lyrics years
    after the fact
anyone whose interpretations are fluid, changeable, interactive, and keyed to
    the marvellous

anyone without envy and resentment
anyone who clearly sees that so much of Western philosophy is an exercise in
    repression
anyone for whom the horizon is an affirmation but not a promise

anyone who has no need whatsoever to contact authorities

VERÓNICA RAZO

If a poem could get to Mexico
If a poem could be a rescue operation
If a poem were an outthrowing of arms

But if this were a world in which
a poem could do these things

it would surely be a world in which
there would be no need for them

and that world is precisely as far
from this one as this poem is from

you, in Mexico, Verónica Razo

HOMEWORK ASSIGNMENT

When you stamp your feet on the pavement, why does the snow come off?
I believe in high standards of excellence and achievement and it is the job of the states to set those standards.

Why is a ballast used in a vessel?
I support great schools—in all forms—and great teachers and school leaders who dedicate their lives to help students achieve and succeed.

Why is a frost more likely with a clear sky than a cloudy one?
Any decision to release information must balance the desire for transparency with mechanisms needed to conduct an appropriate investigation.

Why should a passenger in a canoe sit on the bottom?
The lack of flexibility and adaptability in the system itself is all too often a barrier to success for nontraditional students.

If the lower end of a balloon were left open would the gas begin at once to escape?
These scenarios are perfectly acceptable and in no way suggest that charter schools are unwilling to serve all students.

Why does the presence of an audience improve the acoustic properties of a hall?
Because of this, we must be careful not to brand an entire category of schools as failing students.

What evidence have we that it is impossible to obtain a free magnetic pole?
The model voucher policies include strong accountability provisions.

Why does a blacksmith heat a wagon-tire before adjusting it to the wheel?
It is an idea worth looking into.

Why does sprinkling the floor have a cooling effect on the air of the room?
Fraud should never be tolerated. Period.

Why does the sound of a circular saw fall in pitch as the saw goes further into the wood?
Fraud should never be tolerated. Period.

Why is it possible to get a much stronger current from a storage cell than from a Daniell cell?
We need to work together to find solutions.

Why are utensils used for cooking frequently supplied with wooden handles?
It's the responsible thing to do, especially with taxpayers dollars at stake.

Why is it hard to distinguish between navy blue and black by candlelight?
Let me be clear: Fraud should never be tolerated. Period.

What would be the effect on an organ pipe if it were filled with carbonic acid gas?
Numerous complaint processes exist through the states and courts.

Why does not a mass of liquid air in an open vessel immediately change into gas when brought into a room at the ordinary temperature?
Sadly, too many Americans are suffering from a lack of skills.

How does the temperature of the gaseous products of combustion in the cylinder of a gas-engine at the moment of ignition compare with the temperature at the moment of exhaust?
Additionally, as I have stated, I support equality.

Why are the rails of a railroad track laid with the ends not quite touching?
Calls for free college and debt elimination are in stark contrast with an approach that seeks to address the core challenges in higher education.

Where would you look for a rainbow in the evening?
We need to be sensitive to these situations.

UGLY

Ugly knows it
is ugly and
everything
else. Ugly does
not, cannot be-
lieve otherwise,
but it wants to
find these others
so wise for such
reasons are not
clear to it, but

immediate
and real, like when
in Atlanta
the drive-by boys
call out, "Hey bitch,
I'd like to fuck
you and then fuck
you up," that puts
the gee, oh in
geopoli-
tics—check for ticks—

it's all about
the same place, the
same conflict, star-
ring different
people, because
loneliness needs
no passport. That
everyday
expectation
of disappoint-
ment, ointment for

the skin rubbed raw
every day:
"You don't have to
worry 'bout me."

Whatever the
day of the week,
whatever the
address, Ugly
knows, and ugly
is what ugly
knows.

COVERAGE

We were talking heavily of
the way the world is going
and a fit of inspiration said,
"Frankly, your sky has not been
holding up its end." The silence
that ensued lost the case, maybe
because, hey, the world is every-
thing that is the case, really is
the case, heavy. Heave I must
these surly bonds and so forth
and so fifth. We were talking
of going away. I get what you're
trying to say with that salami
sandwich, just as the pushing
hands of Italian nurses did
eventually get through to me
and when the road says LOOK
LEFT, that's politics. We are
drenched in possibilities but
the towels get changed Tuesdays,
as in each and every. Oh, call me
softcore if you will, but many's
the evening mulls over the tide
over which no blankets may be
pulled. Heavy blankets, very
heaven. When we were talking
of going away, did you mean it,
away, I mean? "Wotta case," pans
the world, with its case packed.

IN THE HALL OF THE MOUNTAIN KING

In the hall of the Mountain King
the browbeaters are busy beating
their breasts. The collector with the
most carrier pigeons has the most
shit, or is that the other way 'round.

Reports are flooding in. Reports are
flooding in. The naysayers are not
saying what they know. Dinosaurs
are making a big splash, coming
and going viral. Just getting this
down. Taking all this in. All this.

In the hall of the Mountain King
there is only the hall, endless hall,
in which you scramble to mean,
what you mean, what you mean.

STUNTS

"So that's what an invisible barrier looks like."
— dialogue excerpt from *Time Bandits* (1981)

A running start
and behind us
the world,

the whole world,

the world too much
behind us, gaining
and losing, never
disqualified, ever
qualified, losing
and gaining on us,

see how now we

fall

behind even
ourselves

A city cleared by a plague,
its trapeze artists are still
not still
but doing
what they do
(close your eyes here,
if you must, and see them
doing what they do,
for I will not *represent* it).

And the tissues take to the streets,
wind in desultory conversation
with the loose forgotten sheets of
some forgotten administration;

but otherwise
no wanderers.

No wonder:
the gasps are gone,
notwithstanding the fact
that there are
still
those who fall
(still with closed eyes
see falling, feel falling
and do what you must,
what you feel you must).

Be lately, as the unknown bird said,
I am flowing up in response to
your application.
This resource cannot be found,
let your hope dwindle,
and jump
from the unwelcoming nest.

What Democritus would say
in this situation: Mutha*fuck*a,
you make me fucken *laugh*.
Or, or Kung. Or Ringo Starr.

A straight face is not a hand;
a straight face is not for lovers;
let us not talk of straight faces,
tonight, let us look neither up
nor down
but watch ourselves doing
this
as though we ourselves were
the ones doing it, this flowing up

without response. Another
kind of application, a whole
other kind, you make me
laugh.

The cops said, "Open up, we are the cops,"
and this is how knowledge happens, when

dinner is over and the dishes washed and put
away again. Goodness, don't you know that

cop shows show what cops are. Once you
have caught on, the dishwasher no longer

seems a mystery or a menace: hear its happy
chug-chugging and know that it, it alone,

is washing the dishes—but from behind
the buckling door the cops can't help adding,

"It'll wash 'em but it won't put them away
again," and what do you know, it won't.

What are we watching?
These streams have been
polluted by an unknown
source. And she (we have
seen her in something else)
has undressed wounds and
unaddressed mail.

But the coordinates don't correspond and

the sink is overflowing. A member of the

custodial staff is red-faced wanting to know

what are

you

trying

to pull

hard

or hard enough

to break, be broken,
break into broken down
hospitals once theatres

with rooms awash in X-rays
of fractured trivia and
dramatis non personae of
covert operas.

I am the treacherous step
long meant to be mended but,

betrayed by our tools,

stays broken, housebroken,
heart, and creaking, heart,
do tread or at least

pull yourself up to

the last floor.

Having to breathe,
        is it convenient?
The allergic imagination

does not so much reply
        as instigate these
sorry throbs in the temple,

varieties of psychosomatic
        experience, all
as if to say: go figure.

Breakfast sorts out
        all sorts of things.
But what chance when

the toast is eaten
        and the day begun
each breath unworried?

Remote the chance,
        but no matter how
but only remote the chance.

Fiction is to the lie as
community is to the state.
Definite articles do reveal
so much: "I love the lamps
but the endtables make
me pout." Into ulterior
decorating? Along the paths
of the Swedish maze of
furnishings await the new
brand of highwaymen, or
so one would like to think.
Right now everybody here is
double-parked. O assoilize,
stuff the passport into the bag
of another and just carry on
carrying on, friends, for those
unfoldable maps are starting

to get ideas.

To fold or unfold

the cartographer says.

Mass and acceleration,

rejoins the physicist.

And the sailor ties on

another:

just you try to

push

a rope

around
whose neck was it?

There is no time
is not on your
bide your time
cunningly, oh this
is not the time
you're looking for.

The neck of time,
clockwise chokehold

What's the damage?

Discuss. Please discuss. No,

duel to the death among the artichokes,
drop your problems and your lists
and have at you!

The backup singers to last night's right-wingers
know how to shake their funny fakers;

a friend's friend's photos of her-
self tindering her affections
give the lie the lay
"je" sans fey avowals—

No more friendly wagers,
       gentlemen's agreements,
       planned communities,
no more.

Clickbait checkmate you push all my buttons
tight butt so what glory glory O Fallujah
holy poop hocus pocus hoi polloi
how poetic, I said, and
regretted it for a long
time afterward.

My magic is not my magic
but yours—
the trick of the magic trick
is to make you mistake
your magic for mine.

For your next trick I

hereby volunteer

to make the audience

jump

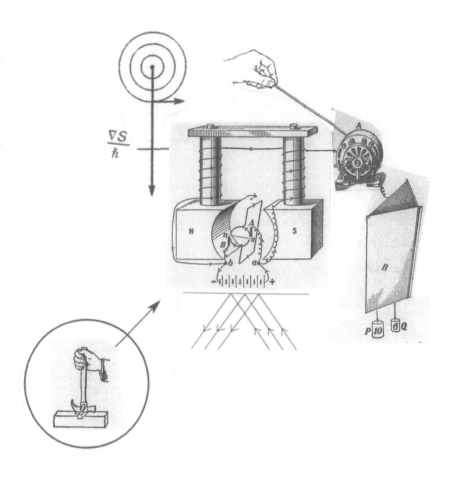

$$\frac{\nabla S}{\hbar}$$

Fig. 140. *Manual generation of hermetic energies.*

SELECTED EXCUSES

1

Jigsaw puzzles are not
courtship and, what's more,
the rules of the game
of tag really don't need
to be written down.

2

I would offer you another generation but
my internet has gone to the beach. At
the time, however, higgledy-piggledy
was very much the thing, it's true.

3

Milk bespilled weeps pointlessly
over the kitchen counter, counting
two three four days weeks months
that words fallen from this mouth
wait like banana peels to blossom
into slapstick, most regretful flora.

4

Break up? Break away.
Unite, Me day, that's
good jungle jargon.
Why wait for the rain
to stop raining? Hurry
down sunshine. We're
what first, and then what
second. Let it never
be said we never
had something to say.

5

Apparently the best Connery
impression rehashes the quip
loosers shay they'll do their besht,
or at least, so I've been told.

6

Never quite made sense how
Herakles killed the Hydra. Not as
a matter of what is, ahem, plausible,
but whether it's cricket or not to have the
information that one head can't be cut off, and
then, what do you know, he cuts it off, just like that.

7

Brimful (pinched it
from Keats) makes me
want to utter
bottomful or
unbrimmed but that
was at the hat
shop and right then
you were trying
on one of your
own chosen hats.

8

The only games worth
cheating at are
those worth playing.
Stake me, take me.

SLAPSTICK II

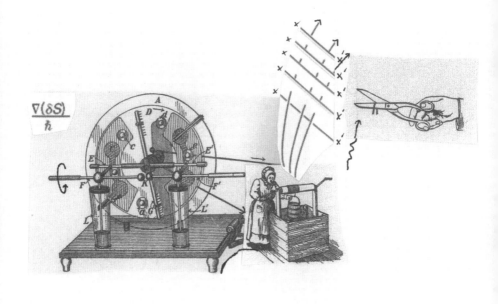

$$\frac{\nabla(\delta S)}{\hbar}$$

Fig. 173 (b). Torque and spin in a confined lifestyle.

AMBITION MEETS HOPE, AMBITION LOSES HOPE

That unfinished story of the
other night has now taken up
residence, Clotho clutching her
head for losing the pattern and
stray cats watchful all around.

An accountant's on the line
wondering where does it hurt:
stall for time, just stall for time
with an eye for some unalloyed
choice cuts of verbal expression.

Glory's gone and good riddance:
there were only so many spurs
to go around. But to invent a
soapdish that doesn't fall, to tie
a knot in fate's thread, estimable!

That was Thursday. Those bastards
took the flick off Netflix that we
were only halfway through but, *but*
we were halfway together. Fractions
matter. I'm not sleeping but dividing.

FOR A SENSE OF A SENSE OF HUMOUR

The laughter of worms,

not easily heard, and
almost never by humans

is low and knowing.
Knowing but not sinister
or bitter, it is always

a collective laughter
a hearty laughter

and how could it not be
with so many hearts in
that innumerable population?

BOUNCE

tension and torque

    ascension and twerk

        assumption and jerk

            consumption and germ

                consummation and charm

                    decimation and churn

                        declamation and cheer

                            destination and fear

                            torque and tension

                      dark and dungeon

                  dart and plunging

              tart and pleasing

          turn and creasing

      tall and crumbling

    fall and tumbling

fate and trembling

THE SALAD BAR AS AN END IN ITSELF

Who's here for spine-
tingling spring tiling?
It gladdens my fervid
salad, bar none, to see,
to sigh. What kinesthetic
kicks are to be had, bald
sir, jingling man oh by
jingo. But wonder where's
the message: maybe cramped
behind the croutons, huh.
Shall a bard sprinkle
dressing, as in Dallas?
All of you with me?
A lad borrows vivid
dreaming from creamy
Italians, clicks so bad
it hurts. But wander
after the message: so
called bingo tomatoes.
Allah'd know, sly boots,
so bold. Tinkled stars
shine for none, all to
scale, a reckoning.

WHAT ISN'T CALLED THINKING?

The living hippo calf being squeezed out of the python;
artistic process.

"I slabbed the segurity in the face," declares the drunk;
annunciation.

Uncontorted expression of the slaughterhouse guest;
objective correlative.

Division of symbol from symptom, that's how
a yawn catches a yawn, the yawn that keeps on
yawning, phenomenology of the quick nap.

And the quickening, inestimable, only seems
comparably perpetual, borborygmic false starts
that will hold dreams close just to refuse them.

MISFORTUNE COOKIES (2 DOZ.)

You are within your rights to seek revenge for what happened Friday. Make it swift and terrible.

—

Next season brings the promise of better blood circulation for you and your family.

—

It is always brilliant to flash your teeth when you smile, but not the way you have always been doing it.

—

Count the exits from this room. The first one you notice is a trap. So are the others.

—

Without a sense of our own insignificance, we cannot expect the stars to notice our intense bowel pains.

—

How delicate, how marvellous is your sense of inadequacy. Cherish it, for it is all that it truly yours.

—

When in life you climb to the highest peak, be sure to be better dressed than you are now.

—

There is nothing to fear from Scottish children, except for that one that you must avoid.

—

Remember that your parents used to be strangers.

—

Darkness is the best friend a compulsive strangler can have, after a good necktie.

—

Your money troubles are not very interesting. You should really get some better troubles.

—

Your success is threatened by your ill-advised love of mountains.

—

Only in the calm silence of night will you come to terms with your nose.

—

Plant roses at the very soonest opportunity, with the knowledge that they will disappoint you in a way that is new.

—

There is no triumph in sitting down without assistance.

—

The person next to you has already betrayed you. Save face and move to Nebraska.

—

Shun butter, buttermilk, butternuts, butterflies, buttonholes, and flying buttresses.

—

If it rains tomorrow, you should call 686-3200 and ask for Liz. Let it ring.

—

Eyes that do not see should be traded in for some truly fine stereo equipment.

—

No one understands your suffering, so it must be extremely important.

—

What great spirits know is that kicking people should be kept to a minimum.

—

The next time your shower nozzle breaks, remember how Napoleon died.

—

To be hungry for the company of people taller than oneself is only slightly laughable.

—

I think about you all the time. My head hurts so much. I think of you and the pills.

ALTITUDE ATTITUDE (KNOCKNAREA)

Do I believe that Queen Maebh stands still,
      under all those stones,
       her sword yet held aloft?

The hike takes us above such questions,
      turn and see significance
       falling behind, below.

FORCE, SHOWS OF

Fig. 205. Approximations of superfluity.

ROUTINE DISRUPTION

The therapists aren't returning calls,
see them running in great triangular formations
into the valleys, unerringly veering together according to
the territory, the open expanses, so majestic as to seem without
purpose, evolutionary or otherwise, for this is their time, time out of

The inboxes have all been folded up
and turned into the ramparts of a great fortress
of virtual cardboard, standing tall and projecting no
small sense of its own imperviousness, though of course its
essential taunts are really wishes for its own eventual collapsing by

The wedding planners spontaneously
combusted, depending on your definition of
spontaneity, but there's no denying the conflagration
they made lit up the heavens not to mention nearly everything
else besides and the heat, jiminy, the word is too paltry, hot enough to

But the ants are making themselves readily available, merrily usurping
the kitchen, all the kitchens, and the brochures about how best to
manage your retirement portfolio and the voice recognition
technology whose kinks are assuredly getting worked
out and the flecks of foam used to cushion subway
seats and the dated bread ties, these all remain
faithful and at hand, they will not migrate
or change, let the waters rise as they
may, these reliable forces abide,

out of mind,
by late rain,
to melt time,
constantly.

HARMED IN THE MAKING

In 1911, a navy cook in Amsterdam
attacked Rembrandt's *The Night Watch*
with a knife.

In 1913, an art historian in Moscow
struck Ilya Repin's *Ivan Grozny and His Son Ivan* three times
with a knife.

In 1914, a suffragette in London
took a meat cleaver
to Velázquez's *Rokeby Venus*.

In 1956, a man
threw a rock
at Da Vinci's *Mona Lisa*.

In 1978, a man in Amsterdam
attacked Van Gogh's *La Berceuse*
with a knife.

In 1985, a man in Russia
threw acid
onto Rembrandt's *Danaë*
and then cut it twice with a knife.

In 1987, a man in London
fired a sawed-off shotgun
at Da Vinci's *The Virgin and Child with St. Anne and St. John the Baptist.*

In 1988, a serial vandal in Hamburg
splashed acid
on three paintings by Albrecht Dürer.
The same man
had previously attacked paintings by Rubens, Rembrandt, and Drost.

Also in 1988, a man
attacked Barnett Newman's *Who's Afraid of Red, Yellow and Blue III*
with a knife.

In 1996, an art student
vomited in carefully chosen primary colours
on paintings by Raoul Dufy (in Toronto) and Piet Mondrian (in New York).

In 2007, a man in Milwaukee
stomped
on Vannini's *The Triumph of David.*

In 2009, a woman in Paris
threw a mug
at the *Mona Lisa.*

In 2011, a woman in Washington
attempted to tear Gauguin's *Two Tahitian Women* from a gallery wall and
pounded it with her fists.

DESIGNATED DRIVE

Instructive to be on a spaceship with
the author of *Trilce*, both of us trying
to recall the details of a movie we have
both seen, at different times, of course,

when the matter of our destination, our
mission's mandate, suddenly arises
and with it the realization that neither
of us knows more about that than about

the forgotten film; but Vallejo tries to
laugh it off, and is that admirable? or
pathetic? or is it a mask, behind which
is Oppen, whose laughter is somehow

very nearly unimaginable, though I can
so readily summon to mind the distinct
laughter of everyone that I have ever
loved, not that such facility necessarily

means anything to yonder control panel,
perhaps misnamed, now flashing and not
flashing, showy and petulant or certain?
or pathetic? or might not this vessel be

propelled by unconscious what-do-you-
call-it, though that might be too much to
ask, being certain of whether it's getting
away from some maybe semi-catastrophe

or else vaunting to some objective, like
rescuing Chelsea Manning, but hang on,
that's forgetting that she's already out,
way out here, caroming with such speed

as seems to guarantee design, but what
hands are on the wheel, if wheel is the
operative term, never mind how sticky
the question of a return trip's likelihood,

never mind all of what was left behind,
notice that Vallejo never once looks
over his shoulder, the kind of man who
dares the world to stab him in the back

and keeps his jacket straight, both of us
in sequined jackets which presumably
have some special function in deepest
space unapparent to the casual observer

if indeed a casual observer were to be
found out here, unless that's what we
are, but purity's too much and too little
to hope for, like the taste of canned

pears never capable of being what it
once was, and too that movie with the
elusive title, and just then everybody,
I mean Vallejo and I and the hitherto

uncommunicative control panel, all
of us decide the title as it was matters
not at all compared with what it will
be, when we arrive at its great discovery.

OBSERVATION DRECK

Wonders Uatu, limp-armed: is it better
to be bested or worsted? He knows not,
no better than anybody else, and today
is laundry day. Events are well soaked
and spin, spin, spin. Browse an ancient
magazine and let's bust out a hymn:

Weep not for the gardener
weep not for the cleaner
weep not for the travelling coffee salesman
for the silver turn of tomorrow's tomorrow
is betrayed by this booklet of coupons.

See, this is how Linda Evangelista got
started: just when the cataclysm seemed
averted and weary backs turned, a curious
hand picks up the cursed wand and
bang! The Molecule Man is back; cliff-
hanger. None of this means, however, that

The real defining moment, fairly real at
any rate, *are those big conflicts where
everything's at stake*, real and everything,
and where you take a side and show you
hang on, harp on, hurl the harpoon into
that wormhole and kiss the enemy goodbye:

For this sense of purpose, many thanks
for this sleepless witness, many thanks
and many more thanks
and we'll see you
seeing us again
next time.

BODIES IN MOTION

Three ways to change
  accident: walking music
  relative: chest wound heals
  in motion: in motion

Old and familiar now, huh?
You're thinking, oh,
this is going to be easy
think again, buddy

that which directly causes motion
that which is in motion
that in which motion takes place
that from which and that to which it proceeds

Nice and strong, high energy
let's bring some intention to this

(When wood travels, its form does not.)

A mover, a moved, an immovable purpose

You don't need to get as wide as us
You don't have to be as fast as us

(Whiteness is not a motion; whitening is a motion.)

Unaccidental change only in contraries,
in intermediate contraries,

don't forget to breathe

in contradictories

Three kinds of change
    subject to subject
    subject to non-subject: perishing
    non-subject to subject: becoming

(That which is not-white might be a man.)

Impossible for that which does not exist to be at rest

    because it is always moving to become, to come into being
if this counts as motion
since motion occurs in space
and what which does not exist
is not in space

Every motion
a kind of change

Three kinds of motion
qualitative

Welcome to level three, baby
want that heart rate   soaring
    stay with me

      big dynamic stretch

    pick up those heels
your body better be heated up

get as deep as you can into that movement

    up, down, up, down

      control,

quantitative
local

squeeze

very, very hard
but very, very effective

(A man is in motion because he changes from light to dark.)

Don't you dare quit on me
you stay with me right now

motion of motion?
    change of change?
        becoming of becoming?

up, down, up, down, nice and slow

Alteration is the motion in passive quality
Increase or decrease is the motion in quantity

you're going to fly away, aren't you buddy?

Locomotion is the motion in place

we are crushing that core

I know you guys are screaming right now

Together   in one place
Apart   different places
Contact   extremities meet
Between   the change before the last change
Succession   posterior but unique
Contiguous   in succession and touches

Continuous   union of limits

some of you may have injuries
some of you may still be working on
the more explosive movements

Motion, like colour, has specific differences

burn it out

Just as knowledge is a species of apprehension
and a genus including various knowledges,
so motion may be one

knees are coming in,
bang, bang

(When a man ceases walking, the walking no longer is,
but it will again be if he resumes walking.)   *there's no shame in doing this motion*

Every motion is continuous,   *nice and slow on the speed*
but distinct motions may be consecutive   *don't want you slamming down*
when time is continuous

it's all gonna pay off

Motions may be regular or irregular

should be burning

but quickness and slowness are not species of motion

explode and drop

Motions between contraries mean that there are contrary motions

Rest is the privation of motion

you wanted to be shredded, right?

Some becomings are violent
and not the result of natural necessity

this is you time, baby,
make the most of it

and are therefore contrary to natural becomings

shoulders should be screaming right now

Motions and states of rest universally exhibit contrariety

you're dying, girl

(Fire moves up naturally and down unnaturally.)

this is really hardcore

But whereas the velocity of that which comes to a standstill
seems always to increase,
the velocity of that which is carried violently
seems always to decrease

you guys, this is where the magic happens

you've got to fight for it
you've got to fight for it

Coming to a standstill means
the locomotion of a thing
to its proper place

hang on, you're almost done

let's take it up and over

breathe

give yourselves a big pat on the back

Motion finds its true contrary
not in a state of rest
but in another motion

PYJAMAS, PYROCLASM

Now that you're tired of me, now we
can talk: reckon just how straight
the jacket, how near the miss. Now
we can separate the socks, distinguish
latent patterns. When you always ask

"how do I look in this shirt?" it's too
much, even once. Bare, pursuant to
an exit: "I'm going back in the closet,
where men are overcoats." The way
you wear my clothes wore well on

me; fit. And speaking of background
microwave radiation, why extinguish
such wan lights as permit any felon
recidivist opportunities, nay, promises
with eventual reconciliations, the sly

conservation of matter. Laundry and
lava, the same volcanic etymology.
This may be covering the same ground,
my sweet Katia, but ever reshaped
by loving telluric argument's flow.

EDITS

Unspooling,
one wonders
when they sweep
the cutting room floor

and how does
this concern
calculations
of the false age

of earth; one
must wonder
when they don't
correct what we

—or what I—
have gotten
wrong, or dis-
connected
what must be put

together,
crumbs, lint, and
sentiments,
into a dustpan

that one grasps
untroubled
like a fact
beyond dispute,

or almost
so; one must
wonder still,
still unspooling.

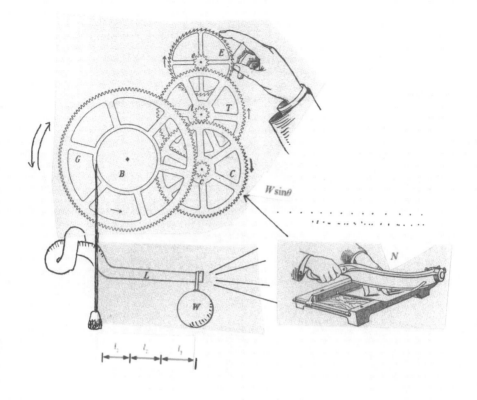

Fig. 232. Unadorned causality momentarily transaccidentated.

NOTES & ACKNOWLEDGMENTS

"Declensions" previously appeared in *Bare Fiction*.

The questions in "Homework Assignment" are taken from *Elements of Physics* (1923), by F. W. Merchant and C. A. Chant, and the answers are those of Betsy DeVos (if such they may be called) to questions from Democratic Senator Patty Murray of Washington, as part of the confirmation of DeVos as U.S. Secretary of Education (2017).

"Stunts" is indebted to H. Netten's sound advice: "There are only two things you need to know: force equals mass times acceleration, and you can't push a rope."

"Misfortune Cookies" originated from an invitation by Stephen Remus to contribute "fortunes" that would be baked into cookies for guests at a dinner to raise funds for the Niagara Artists Centre.

The italicized portions of "Observation Dreck" are taken from a vacuous speech made by a Canadian Prime Minister—I forget his name.

"Bodies in Motion" juxtaposes notes from and dubious paraphrases of Aristotle's *Physics* with verbatim exhortations from Jillian Michaels in her *30 Day Shred* workout video (2008).

I owe thanks to Adam Dickinson, Beatriz Hausner, and Jason Heroux, all of whom read all or parts of this work and offered helpful comments.

This book is for my friend, Stephen Cain.

Tim Conley is the author of four books of short fiction, the most recent of which is *Collapsible* (New Star Books, 2019), and one previous poetry collection. He teaches at Brock University in St. Catharines, Ontario.